THE TURNING POINT, THE LIGHT STILL SHINES IN ME.

Caroline Gallivan

Caroline's experience of Leukaemia
(In her words)

Bright Pen

Visit us online at www.authorsonline.co.uk

A Bright Pen Book

Cover design by James Fitt ©

ISBN 978-0 7552 1096 1

Authors OnLine Ltd
19 The Cinques
Gamlingay, Sandy
Bedfordshire SG19 3NU
England

This book is also available in e-book format, details of which are available at www.authorsonline.co.uk

The Turning Point, The Light Still Shines in Me

I don't know what the future holds. Each day is a gift and every hour and I want to live it to the full.

Chemotherapy is only holding things at bay. I'm not going to be cured but that's where I am at the moment, and life is precious.

Yesterday was Halloween I was with my nieces, they are young and innocent, carefree and they were putting on fancy dress and darting around the room worrying about their face paint not being right. They were excited, as I had been as a child and that innocence was special, and I remembered how I had felt at their age. At five and eight years old they have been told I have bad blood and I am ill. They know about their Granddad who died in the hospice in November last year and they ask me if that is where I will be going they have been told Granddad is sleeping, it's left open and we usually leave the subject.

I want to write my story down so I can help others face the realities of serious, life threatening illness. Particularly focusing on my group (20-30 year olds) and communicate my experience with health professionals to help them become more aware of the trauma arising with leukaemia treatment and care.

I was diagnosed with leukaemia in May 2004 and I've never had a break from hospital - maybe I go once a week and sometimes two or three times. My Mum has been with me every step of the way. In October 2004 I was taken suddenly very ill and as my Dad was dying in the hospice in Letchworth she was torn between being with me and being with him.

Since I was diagnosed I have only met one young man with Leukaemia, and he died.

In 2003 life was really good I'd just met my boyfriend and I had my own house. Mum and Dad had moved into their new home and everyone was really happy. I was working for a pharmaceutical company and my goals were to move around the company to gain as much experience as I could. I had a lovely group of girl friends and we'd meet up regularly to go to the cinema and go out for drinks. Life was settled and my boyfriend and I had been together for three months it was fantastic, exciting, and new and I was totally in love with him. We decided to go to Paris for a week; we had an amazing time, saw all the sites and enjoyed each other's company so much. I could speak to him about anything. On returning I had a bad cold with nosebleeds and felt ill, and on that Saturday evening my boyfriend and my elder sister Marselene took me to the Lister Hospital where I was admitted for a kidney infection. Christmas was three days away and I pleaded with the doctors to let me out with Mum and Dad. The doctors told me I had a high level of white blood cells and e-coli in my specimen, which they put down to the kidney infection. They agreed to let me out of hospital providing my parents looked after me.

That was the first time white blood cells had been mentioned and it was to be <u>the turning point of my life.</u>

I recovered from the kidney infection with anti-biotics but never felt right. I would go to work but by the time I got home had to lie down on the sofa and would sleep until eight o'clock. I just thought I was run down or getting something.

Then, on a particular day I was at work, I had had a very busy morning, I didn't want to go out at lunchtime but needed to pay in a cheque, so I left my lunch at work, jumped in the car and drove to Letchworth to the bank. As I was rushing around town I felt sweaty and dizzy but knew I had to get back to work. I got into my car drove towards work down the Cambridge road. There were police cars doing vehicle checks, I remember changing gear from fourth to third, I felt I was going to faint so I reached my hand down to open the window, as I did so I must have blacked out, the next thing I remember I was to the traffic lights and thank God I hadn't hit anyone. I managed to get to work, round the corner. Everyone commented on how pale and ill I looked but I had my lunch and a cup of tea and thought I was just hungry. I still didn't feel right so I went to the Doctors; he referred me for blood tests, I wasn't worried and waited a month for my appointment. I remember I went for my blood test, which he arranged on a Wednesday morning, and when I arrived home from work that evening there was a phone call from my Doctor to say that my blood results were back and I needed to go to the Lister Hospital and have more tests and a bone marrow biopsy done.

I was in complete shock when I put the receiver down, locked my front door and went straight over to my parents and told them what had just been told to me. They kept telling me not to let my mind get carried away but I could see it in their faces that they were worried and that something was wrong. That evening I sat with my Dad's medical books and whilst trying to convince myself that it wasn't serious when I knew that it was. So the next day I tried to go into work but when explaining the situation to my boss I became really upset and he sent me home. I drove to Mums, left the car and she took me to the Hospital. I went to level ten, the nurses handed me two coloured forms and told me to go to pathology to have bloods taken. As Mum and I stood in the lift I looked at the forms, and in the right hand side it had CML I knew what it stood for I said, "oh God, Mum, Look!" but she smiled and said not to panic, and stay positive.

After my blood samples had been taken I went back to the clinic and waited to be seen. We didn't have to wait long, and were called in by a nurse as we entered the room the consultant a short lady with narrow eyes told us to sit down, a Macmillan nurse was also present. The Consultant asked what my Doctor had said to me and I told her he had said my white blood cells were acting strange.

She looked up at me, and said that we were dealing with something more serious, and that I had Chronic Myeloid Leukaemia. Mum grabbed me, cuddled me and we both screamed into each other's arms. I was numb; it was if time had suddenly stopped, I felt physically sick. She spoke to us about what was now to happen; the drugs to be prescribed and that I must have a biopsy now. The biopsy was the most excruciating pain I had ever experienced and I felt relieved when it was over. Mum drove us back to my parent's house and I broke the news to the rest of my family.

A really weird thing happened to me. Shortly after I had been diagnosed with leukaemia and three months before I had the acute episode, which resulted in my going into hospital very ill, I had an incredibly vivid dream. In it my Dad was becoming sicker and sicker, and I would be rushed into hospital and whilst I was there my father would die. This is, in fact, what did happen.

For a while I avoided my illness, I just carried on, getting up for work despite intense tiredness, and visiting my Dad most evenings after work. I was like a hamster in a wheel that had to keep going. Whilst I had the energy to carry on with my normal life I wasn't ill.

Then in October 2004 my life was going to change. I had got up as normal for work knowing that I had to go to the hospital early afternoon for an appointment. I'd received a telephone call from the Secretary of my Consultant on the Sunday saying something wasn't right and that the Consultant wishes to see me the following day.

I was feeling really ill, I had severe pain from the bone marrow biopsy site and all down my right leg I had excruciating pain, as if it was almost pumping.

How I drove to work that day I don't know. I carried on doing what I could and as normally as possible and at ten o'clock I left said goodbye to my work mates and said I'd see them in the morning. Everything was left as if I'd be back the next day. I drove to my parent's house to pick Mum up as she was coming with me. My sister Fiona was to take my father shopping in Hitchin to buy my mother a birthday present. Mum wasn't able to drive as she had a bad migraine. I drove, parked at the Lister Hospital, went and had my bloods taken and waited to see the Consultant.

The waiting room was quiet; there was hardly anyone around. I kept seeing my consultant walk back and forth from the office, she didn't acknowledge me and made no eye contact and I felt so worried. Eventually another lady who I hadn't seen before came upstairs. I didn't know who she was but something told me it was a Macmillan Nurse. I knew the news was not going to be good. When I'd been diagnosed with leukaemia the Macmillan Nurse had been present. The consultant eventually called me in, we sat down, and she asked me how I was feeling. I told her about the pain and that I was tired. The Consultant seemed to hesitate, as if she couldn't believe the blood results she was looking at. I asked her to tell it to me straight. She explained to me that the chronic myeloid leukaemia had turned into the acute phase. I burst out crying, Mum cuddled me and she cried. When I finally stopped sobbing, I asked what would now happen and I was told I must go straight to hospital for chemotherapy. My leukaemia was out of control and hence the reason for the pain.

The Consultant then said that she had already been in touch with the Royal Free and a bed was available for me, I must go that evening. I was very, very scared and shocked. I pleaded with her to let me go to Ireland, on a family holiday Mum had planned as a surprise for my Dad, but she said I was too ill and had to have hospital care.

The Macmillan Nurse took Mum and I to another room, made us tea and I rang everybody. When I phoned Fiona I asked her not to tell Dad. I wanted to lie to him, tell him I had an infection and that is why I had to be hospitalized I didn't want to worry him.

We sat talking with the Macmillan Nurse; she was comforting, as if she could empathize with us. Fiona phoned to say that Dad had had a small personal accident at her home and so Mum and I left the hospital. I felt completely numb. I don't remember how I got back to Letchworth I did the actions of driving, that's all I can recall. We went to my sister's home Dad was there eagerly waiting for us and I looked him in the face and smiled as if everything was O.K. Mum sorted Dad out. It was just the worst thing telling him.

I dropped Mum in town so that she could buy some things for me and I took Dad back to his home, he didn't want me to go but I had to so I could get things ready to go to hospital. He kept crying and saying he loved me. I went home and put some things in my bag. I have no idea what I was packing. I had previously arranged for the engineer to come and service the boiler, he came bringing a touch of normality into a confusing situation. At eight thirty my brother in law Mark, and Mum arrived.my boyfriend was already with me. (my boyfriend and I had been together for a year and a half; he is my strength and best friend) My bags were packed into the car and I stood in the entrance of my home looking around not knowing if I'd come home. We drove to the Royal Free Hospital.

My bags were unloaded, Mum and my boyfriend took me in, my brother in law hates hospitals and stayed in the car. They walked on either side of me towards the entrance; I said I couldn't go in. It felt as if I was saying goodbye to the world. They encouraged me and we went in and up to the ward. I had never been on an isolation ward before, only read about them in books. We came out of the lift and through double doors, in front was a long narrow corridor with heavy brown doors all shut and the blinds at the windows drawn. I began to cry, it was if I was going into prison.

I was admitted onto a four-bedded bay. We met the nurses and doctor. The doctor filled out forms; a name band was put on my wrist and a canula stuck in the back of my hand so intra venous fluids could commence. Oh God I hated it.

It was about ten o'clock by now, I couldn't comprehend that that morning I had been at work and now I was in a London Hospital. I was so scared and frightened.

Mum and my boyfriend left, I felt desolate and cried into my pillow. Then something nice happened, the lady in the next bed started to talk to me, her name was Kim, and the nurse made us a cup of tea.

Kim was in the same bay for three days and from the moment I was admitted she was an unbelievable support and incredibly caring. I will never forget her kindness. We are still in contact, sadly her eye site is deteriorating and she will become blind in time, she also has to face major surgery. In the meantime she lives in a ground floor flat in London cared for by her parents who live round the corner from her and Kim cares for her two-year-old daughter Chloe. Kim and I met at the most crucial time of my life, she is a dear friend and over the coming weeks she would visit me. I always enjoyed her visits, I wasn't always comfortable when my other friends came to see me, maybe it was the fear of infection or that they didn't understand what I was going through but I appreciated their kindness in coming to see me.

I stayed in the bay for seven days, I was told a single room had become free, room number eight. and my boyfriend was with me, Fiona and Mark had bought Mum and Dad up so I could spend time with Dad. I was often so drugged up all I did was sleep, but Dad sitting in his wheel chair would hold my hand. We waited all morning for the room, then in the early afternoon the hospital staff came round and shut everything, all the curtains were pulled around the beds, the doors shut, and I knew someone had died and they were removing the body. I completely freaked out. The reality that someone had died was too much I was crying, screaming I wanted to stop everything and go home. The nurses realized what was happening and within half an hour I was moved to what was to become my room. They didn't even clean it. They wanted me out of the bay I felt safe in room number eight. Mum decorated it with cards, I looked at the colours and designs it was comforting to know people were thinking of me. When in isolation no fresh flowers or fruit are allowed. Mum brought me some artificial one's bright red poppies and we put them on the windowsill. I had my own television, video and bathroom. I felt sort of safe because there were only 'my germs' and not the wards in the room.

Leukaemia is an isolating illness, most of the time, in fact all, one is nursed in isolation and shut away in this tiny room where everything is dark, the staff always gowned, masked and gloved. The room I was in was small, clinical, cold, plastic beds, pillows and machinery everywhere. The room painted white with brown thick doors, no pictures on the wall just a pin board where I put my cards. The windows were small, with little light and the pane of glass dirty; looking out over London the whole area was grey, the factories, the smoke and no light. It felt there was little life left. The only colours I remember was when the hospital porters pushed the clinical bins and I saw the tops of the yellow clinical waste bags, even the uniforms of the porters were sludgy green and dull.

Adjacent to my room was the preparation, gowning area where the staff and visitors changed to come into my room. As I lay in bed through the dark door that separated us, there was a tiny slim window with a blind and if I got myself in the right position I could see them coming in. I knew they wanted to learn about me – was it me, or were they only interested in my illness? When the Professor came there could be up to twelve other medics with him. They all entered my room pushing around the bed, huddling to fit in. They all held papers, files and bleepers often went off. They wore 'normal' clothes, and each wore a plastic apron and had gloves on, sometimes they wore masks. They didn't look scary but I felt like an alien, someone that was so ill and diseased they wouldn't come near me, as if I wasn't a human being. The Professor was the only one to speak to me and then would dictate to the throng in medical terms that I didn't understand and they would be scribbling something down. I then had to ask and the professor would explain. The only warmth I felt, when I was so ill was when the Professor smiled and said he'd see me next week or on the next ward round, that gave me a tiny amount of hope. After they left my tiny room, I felt empty, scared, lonely (very, very lonely) and because I was neutropaenic (lack of white blood cells). I constantly asked what my bloods were doing so I could get out of the room. It took forever.

I willed my cells to come back so I could get out. I felt imprisoned, and the longer they took to improve the weaker I felt. I had no energy, my legs, arms wouldn't work, my ankles were sore and my skin seemed to just hang. I thought I was sinking more and more into the bed and because I wasn't moving around I was becoming flatter. My muscles wouldn't work, and I thought if only I could get out of here I'd get stronger.

The last time I was to see my dear Dad was 31st October, my Mum's birthday. My sister Samantha and her husband brought them up to visit. Looking back I regret this day so much. If I'd known this was to be our last time together I would have tried to be awake more but every time I opened my eyes my lids they felt so heavy and I had to close them. I was heavily drugged, I didn't want to be awake, nor in the land of the living I wanted to be asleep and not know what was going on. Time was getting on, it was time to say goodbye, Samantha and Gary kissed me and left the room.

Dad became agitated in his wheel chair, he was towards the end of my bed, and wanted to come closer to me. Mum moved the bed table out of the way and also my drip stand, to make more room and pushed the wheelchair to my side. A short time later Mum said it was time to go, I woke up and Dad reached out his hands and held my hand tight, he told me how much he loved me, and that I had to keep fighting for him, they were the last words he said to me, I was so tired and once they had left the room I fell back to sleep.

Dad was admitted to the Hospice the next day for respite but his condition deteriorated rapidly and Mum and Marselene were with him when he died on the 11th November, which was also my boyfriend's birthday and Remembrance Day.

I remember the 11th November so well. My sister Samantha and Fiona came to see me, as well as my Uncle (dad's brother) whom I hadn't seen for years. My sister Marselene phoned to tell us that Dad was dying, Samantha and Fiona started crying and I shouted for them to leave. They both kissed me and flew out of the door. My boyfriend and I sat in silence. The phone rang I thought it was Mum, to tell me Dad had passed away but it wasn't, it was Fiona to tell me because of an accident they were stuck in traffic. The call came from Marselene at 7.12 p.m. Dad had died. I was crying, felt numb and I knew then, from that moment my family would never be the same again.

Only my boyfriend visited after Dad died because the rest of the family were busy notifying other people and arranging the funeral. They would constantly telephone me though To let me what was going on and ask what I would like for the funeral, to be honest I was in a complete trance, words would just come out of my mouth, I couldn't believe it was my Dad's funeral we were talking about.

On the day I was discharged my boyfriend came to get me, we packed up my things in a suitcase knowing they were only allowing me ten days out, I hated this place so much and yet I was scared to leave but I knew I had to and my boyfriend took my bags and put them in the car, and got me a wheel chair. I'd lost so much weight, and all of my hair. I didn't have the energy or muscle strength to walk far. I went outside, the first time for over a month I felt the fresh air on my face. It was amazing and I felt as if I could breathe again.

I can't really remember the journey home as the outside world seemed alien to me and I was so tired I was completely dazed, as if I didn't belong anywhere. We were going back to my parent's house. As we got nearer to Letchworth I began to get stomach cramps and nervous. It was nice being back at my parent's house again but now things had changed. We pulled up outside the house. My boyfriend helped me walk the short distance from the car to the front door where my Mum and sister came to greet me, they hugged and kissed me, and I made my way through to the sitting room. There were cards and flowers and Mum had a beautiful photograph of Dad in a frame, next to it candles were burning. Everything was so peaceful and still. Dad was missing from his chair.

The next day I wanted to see Dad so Mum took me to the undertakers at Baldock. I was so nervous and scared of what he would look like. The lady showed us to this little room outside and as we entered, it was freezing cold inside and behind a lace curtain lay my Dad in his coffin. Mum held my hand, told me not to be scared, it was my Dad and we walked slowly up to him. Mum spoke to him, and told him she'd brought me to see him. He looked absolutely lovely, peaceful and had this gorgeous little grin on his face. I reached down and took his hand it was so cold I just stood there crying. It was horrible. I visited Dad two days later again, and took a photograph of my boyfriend and me, so that he wouldn't forget us. The following day was the funeral, lots of people came, it was an extremely difficult day but we gave my Dad a beautiful send off.

Slowly, I had to prepare myself for going back into hospital. I had gained a little weight, was eating more and feeling a little stronger but I was dreading what lay ahead of me. My boyfriend and Mum took me back; I had a room already waiting for me. This time I wasn't as frightened as I knew the set up and all the doctors and nurses. It was almost like going home!!

The next three days were horrendous. I had to be transferred twice a day from the Royal Free Hospital to University College Hospital, and back again, by taxi to have radiotherapy. I was woken at 5am in the morning to be given a pre medication and a piece of toast, then make my way to the hospital entrance to get in the taxi (needless to say it wasn't always there) and I was taken to University College Hospital.

The treatment was ghastly, I was strapped to the bed and Vaseline packs put all around me. The bed was metal and cold and my arms were tied down and I had this plastic box thing around my head it was terrifying. I was cooked for seven minutes on each side, and I felt so ill. After the treatment I was taken back to the Royal Free and slept most of the afternoon, then at 3p.m. another pre medication would be given to me, and again by taxi I would go for the second dose of the day, returning again by taxi to the Royal Free at about 7 p.m.

My Mum and my boyfriend shared the trips with me. I was utterly exhausted, sick and my skin sore. I felt as if my whole body had been burned. By the third day my head hurt and it too felt as if it had been burnt.

On one of the days it was snowing which made the whole experience even worse as it was really cold and having no hair just added to the discomfort despite my hat!

Having been cooked for three days they then told me I had to have one further dose of chemotherapy before the transplant. This chemotherapy had to be given over a period of four hours, it had the potential complication of affecting my heart rhythm, and so I had to have it on the cardiology ward. I shared the room with four other women all of whom where a bit loopy and I felt I was in the funny farm. I lay on the bed with the curtains around me Mum and a nurse attached me to a heart monitor, the infusion was started. A nurse had to sit with me the whole time watching for arrhythmias, I slept for the majority of the infusion, but unfortunately the last part of the infusion sent me into a really bad rigor and I vomited everywhere. Once I had been stabilized and everything was all right I returned to my room and I slept.

Article by kind permission of Archant Newspapers

Pictured Left to right Fiona, Samantha, mum Stella, Marselene and Caroline

16

Doctors' hope after sisters help in bone marrow search

By TRACY FIELDS

A **YOUNG woman has received the ultimate Christmas present from her sisters this year -the gift of life.**

Caroline Gallivan, 24, was diagnosed in May with chrome myeloid leukaemia.

She was receiving treatment at London's Royal Free Hospital but she deteriorated in October when her condition developed into the far more serious acute myeloid leukaemia.

Doctors began to search for a bone marrow match to Caroline and when testing the whole family they found that elder sister Samantha Newson was a perfect match.

Last Thursday, mother-of-four Samantha went through the painful operation to donate the bone marrow, which was given to Caroline.

The family now faces a wait to see if the bone marrow has "taken" but doctors now say they are hopeful that Caroline's condition will greatly improve.

Caroline has three sisters, Samantha, 39, Fiona, 36, and Marselene, 29. Marselene also gave white blood cells twice to aid Caroline's treatment.

But the positive news from Caroline has been tinged with sadness as the girls' father James lost his own fight with cancer last month.

The girls' mother Stella, 60, said: "It was an extremely emotional moment. Samantha was very ill as well but the hospital were able to put her in a wheelchair with oxygen and take her to Caroline's side because she desperately wanted to see Caroline receive the marrow:

"We all sat around with Caroline as it happened - it was so emotional.

'The doctors say it is very promising. We have a 10 day wait from the transplant to see if the marrow has taken which we will know if her white blood cell count comes up.

"This is the gift of life - without it Caroline would not have lived."

Caroline lives in Letchworth GC and is a former pupil of the town's St Thomas Moore School and John Henry Newman School, Stevenage.

The Anthony Nolan Trust can be contacted on 01865 875757.

My eldest sister Samantha was admitted to hospital, as she was my donor. Despite being really scary it was very exciting as well. Mum made sure Samantha was settled. Unfortunately, they couldn't put us on the same ward; she was on a ward a few floors up. The day seemed to drag on and on and we spent the day talking, watching television and trying not to think too much about what lay ahead. The following day was to be the transplant, Samantha was the first down to theatre, and we waited anxiously to hear if they had managed to collect sufficient bone marrow cells for the transplant to go ahead. The Consultant came in and informed me they had plenty of cells and although my sister was a bit groggy she was fine. Apparently, Samantha didn't sleep much after the operation she wasn't even sick after the anaesthetic instead just tucked in and ate jam rolly polly!

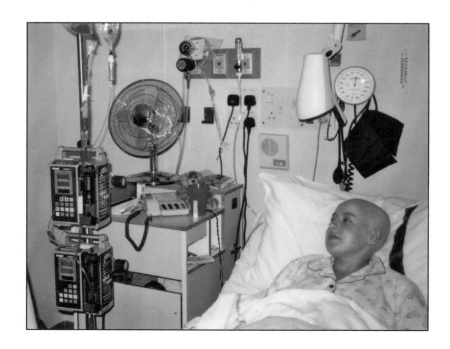

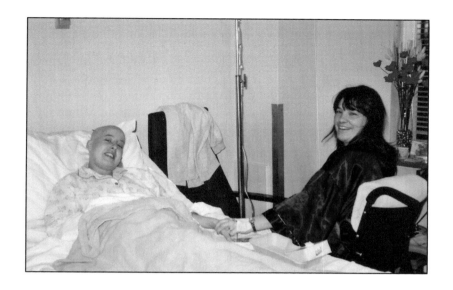

The cells were taken straight to a specialist laboratory where they were spun and prepared for me. The cells have to be transplanted within four hours of collection.my boyfriend , my sister Fiona and my Mum were all with me, Marselene my other sister couldn't be there but Samantha despite a lot of pain insisted on coming to my room, she was put in a wheel chair and was on oxygen. The bag of cells finally arrived; they looked like lightly coloured blood, in a large squishy bag. The consultant hung the bag on the drip stand, attached the cannula to my Hickman line and the infusion was commenced. We all watched anxiously as the cells slowly dripped into me. Samantha was beside my bed in her wheelchair and we held each other's hand and cried. I remember the transplant took place on a Thursday. The same day Dad had died and I was hoping he was up there watching over us all. Mum and my boyfriend busied themselves taking photographs and within half an hour the bag was empty and the transplant was complete.

We all felt such great disappointment that we had all gone through so much for an infusion to be over in thirty minutes!

Samantha returned to her ward as she wasn't feeling too great, Mum and Fiona went with her and my boyfriend and I just held hands and I drifted off to sleep.

Samantha went home the following afternoon, Gary and their children collected her, and I desperately wanted to leave hospital with them.

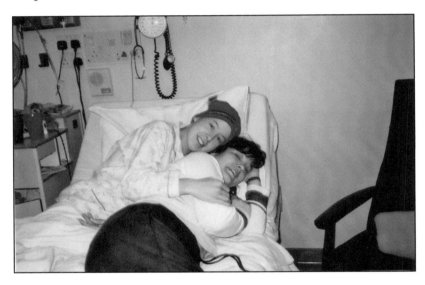

After the transplant I was given anti rejection drugs and infusions, which made me, feel very sick and weak. One of the infusions was called Methotrexate and I had to have four of these, and each time they gave it to me I suffered from inflammation of the mucous membrane in my mouth which was extremely painful and my mouth was full of ulcers and my saliva was like wall paper paste. Christmas was fast approaching and I was told that I would not be allowed to go home for Christmas or the New Year, and although this was terrible there was a part of me which didn't mind as I knew Dad was not going to be there, outside waiting for me.

Mum was fantastic she brought in tinsel, little snowmen and Santa's and decorated my room. It looked like Santa's grotto! Through sheer determination I forced myself to eat and drink, despite my mouth being so sore. Four times a day I would use the mouth washes which were vile, and try to wash my teeth to make sure I got no infection in my mouth.

I can honestly say that this was the hardest point of my illness. I cried every day because of the pain. I was on diamorphine which made me hallucinate and speak gibberish and the only thing that kept me going was the thought that Christmas Day was round the corner and Mum had made me my favourite pasta dish and I was determined I was going to eat it.

I woke really early on Christmas morning my Mum helped me shower at 6.30am. Whilst in the shower one of the Doctors came to see me and told me that my sister's cells had grafted. I just cried, this was the best Christmas present I could have wished for.

A few hours later my boyfriend and his father came to visit me with lots of presents. My boyfriend looked gorgeous, he was wearing a suit and shirt and tie, and he said he wanted to make an effort for me. He had previously shaved all his hair off when I'd lost mine!

I managed to slowly eat my pasta, which I was pleased about and later on in the evening my sister Marselene, and her husband Darren and my niece Kaitlyn came to visit us. Marselene had packed a small Christmas dinner in a lunch box for me to taste. As it was getting late they all had to go and Mum and I were left feeling quite lonely despite having had a nice day.

I don't ever want to be in hospital again for Christmas, it brings back so many memories, you think of the Christmas' you've had as a young child and all the families enjoying themselves and you are stuck in a room. Mum found it very difficult as well and went for several walks. The following week was fairly uneventful; I was slowly getting stronger and getting more used to the drugs. On New Years eve my boyfriend came to see me, it was wonderful to see him but I felt deeply depressed, I got into bed at about 10p.m. and stayed awake to see Big Ben chime midnight I didn't feel happy at all, just lonely and emotional, Mum couldn't stand it and left the room to go for a walk and my boyfriend and I were left just sitting there thinking of my Dad and my boyfriend Mum who had died of cancer, just six weeks before my Dad.

I was discharged the following week and had to attend the clinic each week for my bloods to be checked. With a bone marrow transplant you have to wait 100 days to know if the transplant has been a complete success. I reached 98 days, it was March by this time and I was doing really well, felt stronger, had less pain and felt positive the transplant had worked.

Then it all went terribly wrong. I went for what I thought was a routine clinic appointment and as I was in the waiting room I was called to go and see my Consultant in his office. I can remember walking towards his office feeling that something was not right. The corridor seemed to go on forever and I kept focusing on the white and blue stripes on the floor that lead you to other departments. Once we'd reached my Consultants office he asked my Mum and I to sit down, there was also another junior consultant with him. I could sense their body language it was really uneasy and I knew they had bad news to tell me. My Consultant started explaining about the transplant again, and the hundred days, I was on ninety-eight and he said my Leukaemia was not controlled the transplant had been unsuccessful. I looked straight into his eyes to see if there was any hope, but his eyes were blank, there was nothing there. My Mum started to cry and hugged me. I started to cry too, I felt sick as if everything I'd been through had been a waste of time. I also felt bad for my sister and everything she had done for me. I just felt completely empty. The Consultant then explained that he was not clear what type of Leukaemia I had, I would need to have more tests, and he just knew it had returned. He spoke of a trial I might possibly go on, a new tablet from America, but in order to meet the correct criteria I would need to have a particular chromosome, he explained that he was to use the bloods he'd taken that day and for me to come back the following week. The hospital ordered my Mum and I a taxi, so that we didn't have to go home by hospital transport we sat in silence until we got home.

The following week Mum and I went back to the day centre at the Royal Free and waited to be seen by the Consultant to find out what my bloods had shown. We waited the majority of the morning, eventually we saw the Consultant and he explained that the bloods had not shown the necessary chromosome, and I was probably not suitable for the trial. The Hammersmith Hospital had however agreed to see me and run their own tests.

Throughout my illness I have always wanted to know up front what the situation is. I turned to my Consultant and asked if I wasn't put on the trial how long would I have to live, he answered, that obviously it was difficult to say but most likely about a month. I respected his honesty; at least I knew what I would be facing. My poor Mum couldn't handle it and walked out of the room and started crying with the nurses. Meanwhile I had been in touch with my boyfriend and told him the news and within a couple of hours both he and his Dad were beside me.

Nothing more could be done at the Royal Free, I was due to see the Consultant at the Hammersmith the following week to discuss the possibility of going on this new trial drug.

The days leading up to the appointment were hellish. I knew I needed this particular chromosome to be present in order to qualify for the trial. My boyfriend took Mum and I down to the Hammersmith Hospital, it all felt very strange and different I was out of my comfort zone. The nurses took my bloods and weighed, measured me, and wrote it all in a yellow folder. I waited to see the Consultant, he was this tall, big hairy Spanish guy and really nice with a truly caring persona and very positive. He explained the chromosome I needed was present in my blood, despite being low and I was able to qualify for the trial. This was such good news I could have screamed. It was like a tiny flicker of light had come into this dark tunnel. We discussed all the implications of being on the trial. The tests that would need to be done, and I also met the two research nurses that would be looking after me whilst I was taking the drug. They gave me all the relevant paper work and the diary I would need to fill in and then gave me the containers, which contained this 'miracle' drug. I was feeling really nervous and apprehensive about starting this new treatment. I was excited too. It had given me hope and where there is hope there is life.

I continued on the drug for six months and despite having bad side effects and infections it put my Leukaemia into remission, sadly at the beginning of October 2005 the drug stopped working and I was with drawn from the trial. I felt completely devastated and once again the light in the tunnel had gone out. I was so fed up with bad news and coming close to death all the time. I felt like giving up the fight. My Consultant always stayed positive though and said there were other chemotherapies they could give me to keep things at bay and that I must continue to stay positive. He told me that if another trial came up that he thought I would be suitable for then he would put me on it. He said he could transfer me to my local hospital if I would prefer but I wanted to stay at the Hammersmith where I felt safe. Although I haven't been attending the Hammersmith for the length of time I was at the Royal Free, it has become almost like a second home to me.

Every Monday I go to the Hammersmith, I get up at about 5.30am and the transport picks me and my Mum up at about 7.30am, it's a tiring day, I feel lucky to be under their care. They know me and I know them.

So this brings my story to where we started.
I've had my ups and downs but I shall continue to fight as I promised my Dad when he visited me in the Royal Free on his last visit to see me.

I'm trying to stay as positive as possible and when I'm feeling well enough I do fun things such as tea at the Ritz with Mum and my sisters and shopping in Harrods with Mum. . The Willow Foundation arranged for my family to go to see the theatre production of the Lion King, and we travelled in a stretch limousine, it was a wonderful day. I am hoping to visit Cyprus soon.

I've written this account so that it gives you all an insight into how quickly life can change from being a carefree young adult to one where every day, every hour is precious.

My message is that health is invaluable treasure it, and the love of family and friends is the greatest gift of all.

Caroline passed away peacefully at her Mother's house on the 12th May 2006 with all her family and loved one's around her.

Printed in the United States
1370LVUK00001B